Seasons Of The Soul: Love And Awakening In Kyoto

Estações da Alma: Amor e Despertar em Kyoto.

Glicia De Almeida

BookLeaf Publishing

India | USA | UK

Made with ❤ on the BookLeaf Publishing Platform
www.bookleafpub.in
www.bookleafpub.com

Dedication

To my beloved mother, Francisca Edna dos Santos Castro, whose wisdom, strength, and love shaped the very essence of my being. With love and gratitude.

À minha querida mãe, Francisca Edna dos Santos Castro, cuja sabedoria, força e amor moldaram a essência do meu ser. Com todo o amor e gratidão.

Preface

Season of the Soul: Love and Awakening in Kyoto is a collection of poems written during the decade I spent in Kyoto, a city that forever changed the course of my life. In the heart of Japan's ancient capital, I discovered the power of beauty and imperfection (Wabi-Sabi) while coming to a deeper understanding of myself.

Kyoto's culture, hidden gardens, and centuries-old temples are more than just picturesque—they possess a quiet magic that touches the soul. In the stillness of its landscapes, I found the love of my life, became a mother, and grew both as a person and a scientist. As the seasons changed each year, I too transformed, witnessing the brief yet eternal dance of time inside my mind. The graceful fall of the sakura petals, like fleeting moments; the gentle flow of the Kamo River, side by side in early April—each a reminder of life's passing and its persistence.

This book is a reflection of that transformation—the gradual unfolding of life's deeper truths. Each poem captures the essence of a place where my soul could breathe freely, where love was found in the simplicity of everyday moments. Kyoto taught me that awakening is not a dramatic, sudden event but a gentle, ongoing process—one that is often subtle and quiet, requiring a willingness to be embraced and accepted.

In Kyoto, beauty exists both in the permanent and the impermanent—the shifting seasons, the falling blossoms, the vibrant hues of autumn, and the chill of the melancholic winter breeze. My poems celebrate that same spirit—honoring the fleeting moments, the unexpected discoveries, and the joys of life as a foreign mother and scientist.

As you read these pages, I invite you to experience Kyoto through my eyes—to hear the soft silence of its temples, to see the graceful colors of its changing seasons, and to feel the profound sense of belonging that comes from living in a place so far from home yet so deeply connected to my heart. *Season of the Soul*—a season of love, growth, discovery, and awakening. May these words touch something deep within you, just as Kyoto's beauty continues to live within me.

Acknowledgements

This book is a reflection of the love, peace, and memories I found during my time in Kyoto. It is a testament to the journey I undertook—one that I could not have completed without the guidance and support of so many incredible people, to whom I owe a deep debt of gratitude.

First and foremost, my heartfelt thanks go to Professor Makoto Noda. Your guidance, both intellectual and personal, has been a steady beacon of light throughout my Ph.D. Your wisdom went far beyond the academic; you taught me the power of patience, the importance of humility, and the beauty of seeing the world through a lens of deep understanding. You have profoundly shaped my view of both Kyoto and myself, and for that, I will be forever grateful.

To my dear Japanese friends, thank you for opening your hearts and lives to me. In your kindness, generosity, and quiet wisdom, I found not only lifelong friendships but also the true meaning of connection. The shared experiences, laughter, and stories have woven this chapter of my life into something truly unforgettable. You have shown me that love and peace are found in the smallest gestures, the simplest moments, and the deepest bonds.

This book would not exist without each of you. You have all contributed to the awakening I experienced in Kyoto, and it is with profound gratitude that I dedicate this work to you. Thank you for lighting my path and for being the living embodiment of Kyoto's beauty.

1

. Love to thrive

It is time, oh Mother, to arrive,
To love what exists, to breathe, to thrive.
In the air, in the spaces we cannot see,
Love remains, unshaken, wild, and free.
Against the pull of gravity's fierce hand,
It rises, it stands, unbroken, unmanned.
In the warmth of a mother's embrace,
There's calm, there's light, there's a sacred grace.
With faith, with strength, I loved without end,
Through all the hours, you did not bend.
Oh life, you gave me more than I could ask,
Through the labor, through the love, through a divine
brask
From the certain of our salted years,
We carved our story through joy and beers
A child born within, birthed anew,
In a moment, diluted the blue
It is time, dear Mother, to revive,
To love, to breathe, to feel, to thrive.
In green air, where whispered hopes may be,
Love lingers strong, unshaken, wild, as the sea.
Against the pull of gravity's strong chaos,
It rises, firm, it stands—unbent, unmanned.

Within the warmth of a mother's kiss
A marble leaf fall in peace
With color and fragrance, loved beyond all measure,
Through every hour, your voice is my treasure.
Oh Mum, you hold me in your chest
In later hours wish me the best
From doubt and silent, whispered tears,
We shaped our tale, as perfect spheres
A soul was born within, as rose anew,
And in that hour, I was born too.

Pelo Amor, crescemos

É hora de chegar
De amar o que existe
No ar e sem ar
O amor persiste
Contra a gravidade crua
Não cai e nem fere
Pelo maternal abraço
O teu sol se desperte
Com fé e força
Amei sem medida
Todas estas horas
Que me deste, ó vida!
Da incerteza ao sal
Fizemos nossa história

Filho que nasceu em mim

(Kyoto 2011.07.14)

2. Rocky poem

My poetry rises from the rocks,
Heavy blocks, scattered fragments,
Pressed together in compact hours,
It stirs the dust,
A beauty that lifts me higher,
Hot particles drawn deep within.
At times, wrapped in mystery,
These are the hours reflected beyond my skin,
By actions, human and true,
And the release of what I need to shed.
Part of a whole that shapes each soul,
And when it departs, hard,
Crushed beneath the weight, it rises,
Expands the spirit, carved into the flesh.
I shed my skin, and so many more,
Wrapped in a world that forgets,
To make me lighter, to make me free.
The poetry that flows from me,
Strange and ancient, could be harsh,
As harsh as the trials of my youth,
But no...
It is what stretches wide, at the edges,
A chance to rise above the stone,
To join with the trees,

The beasts, and the roses.

Poema rochoso

Minha poesia se desprende das rochas
Blocos, fragmentos, compactas horas,
Gera uma poeira fina,
Beleza que me ilumina,
Partículas quentes aspiradas pela narina.
Às vezes cheia de mistério,
São aquelas horas refletidas fora de mim,
Pelos atos tão humanos,
E pelas desconstruções de minhas necessidades.
Como parte de um todo que faz cada pedaço do homem,
E quando se despede, duro,
Amargo, reduzido, cresce,
Expande a alma e suas metáforas na pele.
Tiro minhas cascas e tantas outras,
Cobertas pelo mundo que se esquece,
Para me fazer mais leve.
A poesia que sai do meu ser,
Estranha e arcaica, poderia ser dura,
Como foi minha infância,
Mas não...
Ela é o que expande
Em minhas extremidades,
A oportunidade

De ir além das rochas,
Ser parte das árvores,
Dos bichos e das rosas

(Kyoto 2016.05.01)

3. From the top of Hiei

From the top of Hiei
I was thinking ...
When I was born
No angel came to see me,
just the cold bite of pain
My father died
and I grew up with that mark
the guilt gnawing at my gut
like I killed him in the birth.
His days ended with mine still flickering,
fading, while mine were just starting to burn.
There wasn't enough strength in my heart
to reach out, to hold a hand.
We walked alone,
lonely as hell,
pieces of stale bread on a broken plate
crumbs of feelings,
swept away by time,
and the bitterness that crawled into my roots
It turned into poison in my eyes,
crystalized rage
shattered
with the quiet that came slowly,
in every poem,

in every line,
with the ugly beauty of it all.
The rhyme didn't fix shit
but it dulled the ache
spilled out the love
and in my last breath
the angels finally grabbed my hand.

Do topo do Hiei

Cheguei no topo do Hiei
E pensei...
Quando nasci,
Nenhum anjo me visitou.
Nas crespesas das dores,
Meu pai morreu.
E cresci assim,
Com a culpa de tê-lo matado no parto,
Findados seus dias com a luz dos meus.
Faltou força no coração para darmos as mãos.
Andamos separados, guiados pela solidão.
Pedaço de pão mofado no prato quebrado,
Migalhas de sentimentos levadas pelo tempo.
O fel que nutriu minhas raízes
Se converteu em fel nos olhos.
Amargura cristalizada,
Que foi quebrada

Com a suavidade e a calma.

A cada poema,

A cada verso,

A cada linha,

A beleza da rima

Diluiu a dor,

Derramou o amor.

E no meu último suspiro,

Os anjos seguraram a minha mão.

(Kyoto 2016.04.19)

4. Whispers of Wabi-Sabi

In the depths of this shadowed night,
A star rises, lost and longing,
While I, just a traveler, catch a glimpse—
A wasp's flight, swift and untamed,
And there, in the midst of stones and thorns,
A rose blooms, its fragrance bold,
Carrying beauty in a garden of beasts.
And as April's morning spreads its light,
The sun, fierce and radiant, bursts forth—
A promise of life, ever renewed.
Somewhere in Brazil, hope hums its song,
While in Kyoto, the Heian Shrine stands—
Its ancient stones, steeped in wabi-sabi,
A quiet elegance found in imperfection,
Where moss clings to time-worn edges,
And the cherry blossoms bow in humility.
In Brisbane, I sip tea with my aunt,
As we speak the language of time,
Each word a thread in the tapestry of memory.
Amidst the sea of voices,
This humble verse may seem small,
But do not be deceived, beloved reader,
For in your hands rests a truth most sacred:
You, yes you, are a poet divine,

With eyes that see the unseen,
A heart that weathers every storm,
Mended by poetry's golden touch,
Like Kintsugi, the art of mending broken things.
In this vast world, every fragment is part of the whole,
Every stone, every petal, every broken vessel,
An echo of the sacred imperfection that binds us
together

(Shugakuin - Kyoto 2009.05.14)

5. Resilient Sakura

If life was a garden
where sakura blooms,
its petals fragile like a dreams
Carrying the silent beauty
When the wind comes,
When rain falls,
and still, it blooms.
Not for forever,
but for this moment—
a fleeting grace,
a brief touch of divine
before it fades.
Through storms,
through heat and cold,
the sakura sways,
its branches trembling,
but never breaking.
In its vulnerability,
it whispers:
"Here I am,
and I will bloom,
even if only for a while."
I see it there,
in the heart of Kyoto,

where the Kamo River flows,
its waters quiet,
carrying away the blossoms
that fall like forgotten memories.
The sakura's fragility,
like my own fragility,
teaches me that life is not
about how long we endure
but how deeply we live
How we bloom despite the storms
even when the world demands
that we wither
So I under the sakura`s tree,
the clouds flows,
the river flows by my side.
Together, we have no need
for the promises of eternity
We have only the moment.
And in this moment
we are enough
The sakura stands,
and I stand with it,
fragile,
resilient,
and blooming.

(Marutamachi - Kyoto 2010.08.10)

6. Finest Lesson

Spring—
I don't know where it begins,
but I feel it, in the air,
in the Kamo River, in the shrines
of a world I cannot touch with my hands.
It's a color that stirs something inside me,
but it was only in the core of the tree,
that I understood,
understood for the first time,
what it is to truly experience spring.
Winter,
a weight that pressed against me,
I had forgotten what it was to live,
to be alive in a way that feels like waking.
Then the seeds—
the tiny seeds—
the ones I can never see,
they open their eyes,
they blink
and suddenly,
there is light.
No shadows.
No darkness.
Just the sun,

rising, rising, and rising.
The trees,
I can't stop thinking about them.
How they grow,
courageous,
as if it were the most natural thing,
spreading their branches toward the sky.
They dream.
They dream of being something more—
a bonsai, a thing of elegance.
But it's not just that.
There's something more.
A truth I don't know how to explain.
The master tree.
It spoke, as trees speak,
not in words but in the spaces between breaths.
How great could you be, it asked.
How great could you be in a world that's not kind to
growth?
It's not easy, this life.
You wake up and find winter again.
Spring passes.
And what are you left with?
What is left of you when the cold returns?
But the master tree—
it didn't say despair.
It didn't say it at all.

It only said:
Be brave.
Be persistent.
There are seasons—
too many of them.
Too many to understand,
and yet I must live them all.
The hardness?
You fight it.
You fight it because you can't do anything else.
You spread your light,
even if it's only a sliver,
and let it pour into the air.

(Higashioji - Kyoto 2013.01.27)

7. Petals of Being

What is life in the abyss of synapses
 In the organic soup of emotions
 In the covalent bonds to cellular receptors
 In the rational measures and precise calculations of
experiments
 The singular part of the whole that is lost and found
 And there I am
 This thing that breathes
 A being fragmented yet whole
 What is life
 In the culture plate at the incubator
 Relying on salts, sugars, and amino acids
 Are arranged neatly
 Yet do they matter
 More than what cannot be held
 More than the things that pass through us
 Life is magic it is the mysterious light
 A trembling shimmer that is ungraspable
 And so I reach beyond the machines and lab tests
 And I find it
 It is in the flying bird
 In the ties we make and release
 In the smiles we share
 In the words in seed, culturing in someone's heart

Life is beyond the Momiji colors
Life is beyond Hanami hours
It spills out in the light that reflects in our eyes
In the soft silence of the kamogawa couples
This breath and this sounds
This fleeting whisper of being
In petals of sakura unseeing

Kyomizutera - Kyoto (2023.04.16)

8. We Go

We go, hand in hand—
sometimes in steps too small to notice,
sometimes in strides that feel like running,
always beyond the edge of everything.
Hand in hand, we go.
On dark, heavy days,
in nights so clear and endless
that we forget the weight of time,
we go—
in moments that feel certain
and others, uncertain,
but still we go, hand in hand.
Why wait? What are we waiting for?
To wait for life is not to live—
life is movement,
a thousand unspoken dimensions.
A pulse in the chest,
the heart beating,
the years, slipping by—
circular, multiplying.
What light have we carried?
What reflection of the world
did we see in each other?
We go on.

Beyond ourselves,
we go.

Juntos Vamos

Vamos, de mãos dadas—
às vezes em passos tão pequenos que mal percebemos,
outras vezes em passos largos, como se estivéssemos
correndo,
sempre além de tudo.
De mãos dadas, vamos.
Nos dias escuros, pesados,
nas noites tão claras e infinitas
que esquecemos o peso do tempo,
vamos—
em momentos que parecem certos
e outros, incertos,
mas ainda assim vamos, de mãos dadas.
Por que esperar? O que estamos esperando?
Esperar pela vida não é viver—
a vida é movimento,
mil dimensões não ditas.
O pulso no peito,
o coração batendo,
os anos, escorregando,
circulares, multiplicando.
Que luz carregamos?

Qual reflexo do mundo
vimos um no outro?
Seguimos.
Além de nós mesmos,
vamos...

(Shugakuin - Kyoto 2010.02.10)

9. The Last Winter's Leaf

There are days when men are more brothers—
and then, there are days when the hours,
they break. Empty.
The last winter`s leaf, plenty
Life becomes, simply, inert.
Pain, fatigue, fear, injustice, anger—
they arrive too early,
and make their home inside our brains.
Why is pain so much stronger?
Why do the shadows seem to move faster?
If they do, it is because we are lacking something—
a courage we can't quite find
to light up the dark.
We are missing so much.
Sometimes, the only thing left to do
is to be silent in the face of fear.
And in the silence,
when loneliness becomes so present,
we must remember the flowers.
The flowers existing even without a grance.
The insects eating the leaves in the summer heat.
The protein shells that will one day shed.
Everything has a price.
Even fear—

when it paralyzes the muscles,
the body stilled by its weight.
But there is a way.
Because beyond us,
there is an infinite of possibilities
Known as God`s hand

A ultima folha do Outono

Há dias em que os homens são mais irmãos—
E então, há dias em que as horas,
simplesmente se quebram. Vazias.
A última folha do inverno, cheia.
A vida torna-se, simplesmente, inerte.
A dor, o cansaço, o medo, a injustiça, a raiva—
eles chegam cedo demais,
e fazem morada dentro de nossos cérebros.
Por que a dor é tão mais forte?
Por que as sombras parecem se mover mais rápido?
Se assim for, é porque nos falta algo—
uma coragem que não conseguimos encontrar,
para acender a luz na escuridão.
Nos falta tanto.
Às vezes, a única coisa que resta
é silenciar diante do medo.
E no silêncio,
quando a solidão se faz tão presente,

devemos lembrar das flores.

As flores que existem mesmo sem fragrância.

Os insetos comendo as folhas no calor do verão.

As cascas de proteína que um dia irão cair.

Tudo tem um preço.

Até o medo—

quando ele paralisa os músculos,

o corpo imobilizado pelo seu peso.

Mas há um caminho.

Porque além de nós,

existe um infinito de possibilidades,

E este infinito é a mão de Deus.

Shugakuin - Kyoto (2009.06.29)

10. The Light Beneath Our Scars

It is the uncertainties that nourish us,
They offer the essence of the days we live,
For in each day, we learn anew.
Neither men nor women are spared from fear—
In the trembling of my soul, I see it,
We are all the same dust of the earth,
An energy that wears down but also grows.
It is the uncertainties that redeem chaos,
Men and women, with their scars,
Shine under the sun that doesn't ask who we are.
In the light of life, everything shines,
Even these cold tears that fall and teach us.
Beyond the atoms, beyond the wounds,
Love mends what time cannot heal,
The catastrophes that were,
And the ones yet to come,
Are soothed by the soft, patient touch of love.

A luz sobre nossas feridas

As incertezas que nos nutrem,
Oferecem a essência dos dias que vivemos,
Pois cada dia, aprendemos de novo.

Nem homens nem mulheres estão livres do medo—
Somos todos a mesma poeira da terra,
Uma energia que se desgasta, mas também cresce.
São as incertezas que resgatam o caos,
Homens e mulheres, com suas cicatrizes,
Brilham sob o sol que não pergunta quem somos.
Na luz da vida, tudo brilha,
Até essas lágrimas frias que caem e nos ensinam.
Além dos átomos, além das feridas,
O amor remenda o que o tempo não pode curar,
As catástrofes que foram,
E as que ainda virão,
São suavizadas pelo toque suave e paciente do amor.

Sanjo - Kyoto (2009.09.23)

11. Kyoto's Quiet Seasons

I fight with empty hands,
and my heart, it is full of feelings—
too full, too much—
as if it might break from being too full.
I fight against my fragility,
but fragility is so familiar,
it sometimes feels like part of me.
I fight against my weakness,
but the weakness is there,
in every corner of me.
I fight against ignorance,
but is it really ignorance?
Or just a kind of quiet knowing I don't understand?
And the wounds,
so deep,
but I've learned to live with them,
so deep, I no longer know where they start or end.
I fight like a seed fights the earth,
fighting with something as ancient as time,
to open my leaves,
to show something green,
but only to a world so full of gray—
a gray that spreads itself
across everything,

without asking permission.
And no, I do not believe my fight is noble—
not in the way others might say,
in the way others might see it,
as something heroic,
as something that makes sense.
No,
it is not that kind of fight.
It is a fight that comes from the pretension of
transforming chaos
into something beautiful,
but maybe beauty is an illusion,
maybe it doesn't exist,
not the way we want it to.
But there is something,
something divine in that pretension.
Something that makes it feel less like a pretense
and more like a divine act—
a God creating the world
from the chaos,
from nothing,
from the turmoil,
as if He is always beginning again.
Light from darkness,
life from inert matter,
always and forever,
starting over.

I fight against the neglect of space,
spaces that lose their shapes and lines,
falling apart,
falling out of place.
The disorder comes,
inviting dust, fungi,
indifference.
And still,
I fight against the excessive order,
the order that suffocates,
that limits everything that could be,
anything that could grow.
We need walls, yes,
but we also need gates,
gates that open now and then,
so that ideas, feelings, bodies,
they can flow through.
But there is a hesitation,
there is a fear in opening them.
I fight with my own darkness.
Sometimes I grow tired.
I grow so tired of fighting.
But then—
then I see it.
That tiny light.
So small, so fragile,
called hope.

It calls out to my soul:
"Don't stop, girl.
Don't stop now.
Even if it's slow—
keep going.
It will be worth it,
I promise.
Keep going."

(Kyoto 2009.08.07)

12. Where Hope Sleeps

In the depths of night, as hope slumbers on the world's
tired shoulders,
The path ahead, lost in shadow, smolders quietly,
A journey marked by pauses, by pain—
But pain is no stranger to the strong.
Loss leaves behind a kind of grace,
Framed in memories that imprison us.
Rising from the rubble of my broken pieces,
Each fragment, each shattered dream—
No, they are not forgotten.
Isn't it the deepest wound?
The one that burns like fire,
Yet leaves no scar?
We carry it with us,
Invisible.
The muscles that refuse to move,
The rigid fibers that turn to stone—
A testament to how we forget what is life.
Anticipation without action holds no joy,
It chills, it stiffens,
Stillness becomes a prison,
A cage we've built ourselves.
I see without truly seeing,
My heart heavy with a thousand silences.

Yet I move, not hastily,
But with quiet purpose,
To shake off this somber weight—
For deep inside, I know,
Hope does not sleep forever.
Like the earth, burdened by its own groaning,
I wait,
Until the sun kisses the earth,
And fills the air with promise.
The cherries burst into extraordinary bloom,
Coating the mind with their bright pink,
A fleeting vision, but it stays.

(Kyoto 2010.11.03)

13. Seasons of Kyoto

Winter wraps its arms in quiet grace,
The nabe warms the soul, the hearth, the hand,
Family gathers, hearts in soft embrace,
While outside, snow falls like a distant land.

Spring bursts alive with petals on the breeze,
Along the Kamo, we walk in the glow,
Hanami whispers truths beneath the trees,
Where blossoms fall, yet teach us how to grow.

The summer sun is fierce, the air a burn,
Kakigori cools, and cicadas scream,
The koi in shaded pools quietly churn,

In leaves of green, they glide through summer's dream.
Autumn's fire paints the earth with light and sound,
And in its golden hues, we rest, unbound.

Estações de Kyoto

O inverno envolve os braços em suave graça,
O nabe aquece a alma, o fogo, a mão,
A família se junta, corações em abraço,
Enquanto lá fora a neve cai, distante e vã.

A primavera explode viva no ar,
Ao longo do Kamo, caminhamos na luz,
O hanami sussurra verdades sob o olhar,
Onde as flores caem, mas nos ensinam a crescer.
O sol de verão é forte, o ar a queimar,
O kakigori refresca, as cigarras cantam alto,
Os koi nas águas sombrias começam a dançar,
Nas folhas verdes, deslizam pelo sonho do verão.
O fogo do outono pinta a terra com luz e som,
E em seus tons dourados, descansamos, sem pressa, sem
dom.

(Kyoto 2009.09.12)

14. The Silence She Hugs

She paints her face, and that's where it starts,
Like a lie that holds up the world's cheap cheer.
We clap, we laugh, we spill their drunken hearts,
And she nods, pretending she's not here.
Behind the smile, there's a damn empty room,
A bed that stays cold, a heart that won't break.
She hugs the silence, smells the smoke and gloom,
Watches the hourglass slowly shake.
The dinner's done, the fake joy fades away,
And she's left alone, skin tight like a cage.
Another night spent chasing ghosts that stay,
In the spaces where love never engages.
Under the makeup, behind the silk and lace,
She's just another face?
Or we are all lost in this place?

O silencio que ela abraça

Ela pinta o rosto, e começa,
Como uma mentira que sustenta a alegria barata do
mundo.
Aplaudimos, rimos, derramamos seus corações
embriagados,
E ela acena, fingindo que não está aqui.

Por trás do sorriso, há um maldito quarto vazio,
Uma cama que fica fria, um coração que não quebra.
Ela abraça o silêncio, sente o cheiro da fumaça e da
escuridão,
Vê a ampulheta balançar lentamente.
O jantar acabou, a falsa alegria desaparece,
E ela fica sozinha, a pele apertada como uma prisão.
Mais uma noite passada perseguindo fantasmas que
ficam,
Nos espaços onde o amor nunca se envolve.
Por baixo da maquiagem, atrás da seda e da renda,
Ela é apenas mais um rosto?
Ou todos nós estamos perdidos neste lugar?

(Kyoto 2009.11.03)

15. November in Arashiyama

In Arashiyama,
Through the mist, I see your eyes—
My heart finds its home

Warm bamboo leaves,
Solitude meet, soft as river's flow—
Love blossoms in silence.

Arashiyama em Novembro

Em Arashiyama,
Através da névoa, vejo seus olhos—
Meu coração encontra seu lar

Entre as folhas de bambu,
Solidoes se encontram, suaves como o rio—
O amor floresce em silêncio.

(Kyoto 2009.11.22)

16. Garden of Nanzen -jin

I stand in the garden, but I do not stand.
The stones are still, but they are not.
The rake's sweep in the sand—a gesture so small,
and yet the world is drawn in it
The lines
Curves that curve, but who makes them?
Who is the hand that shapes this silence?
Not the rake, not the hand, not even the sand.
It is the space between,
where everything is and is not,
where nothing belongs, and yet it is all here.
I wonder, are these stones aware?
Do they feel their stillness?
Does the sand, so gently raked,
recognize itself as motion?
Or does it, too, rest in the question:
What is it to be?
I see the children
Their feet, running like they belong to the wind—
and yet, where do they go?
What is the shape of their happiness?
The green walls rise,
a simple thing—
trees, moss, leaves—

and I wonder how they know
that they are a wall.
Do they know?
Or do they simply *grow*
And in that knowing, that growing
is there peace?
The temple behind me breathes
It is not the building that breathes
but the quiet.
The walls—old, still,
do not ask to be seen.
They stand because standing is enough.
I hear the silence of a question,
What is this peace?
I have only the feeling of it,
the weight of it,
as though the world were wrapped
in the soft fabric of an invisible hand.
But the hand is not there.
The children run.
Their laughter—sharp, high—
cuts through the stillness,
but even their sound is fleeting.
It will pass,
as I will pass.
But in this moment,
in the space between the sound and the silence,

we are here.
Not forever, but here.
Not named, but here.
The garden waits.
And I, too, wait,
without knowing what for.
The rake sweeps.
The children run.
The walls stand.
And the peace?
It is not a thing you hold,
but a thing you let go of.
And in letting go,
it becomes you,
it becomes me.
We are nothing,
and yet everything.

(Kyoto 2014.06.19)

17. Maiko

In my neighborhood, Maiko walk in thrall,
Her silk-clad form aglow against the dusk,
Cherry blossoms bow, they hear the call,
And Kyoto hums in silence, soft and just.
The lanterns flicker, casting light on air,
Her sleeves like rivers, flowing free,
Each step a song, a prayer, a soul laid bare,
As time bends low and dreams take up the skies.
The air is rich with incense, warm and deep,
A scent of grace, of truth, of what we seek,
While shadows stretch, like whispers we must keep,
And stars above bend low, their voices meek.
Kyoto, in this night, so soft, so bright,
Maiko's beauty shines, a beacon, a light.

No meu bairro, Maiko caminha em encantamento,
Sua figura de seda brilha contra o crepúsculo,
As cerejeiras se curvam, ouvem o chamado,
E Kyoto murmura em silêncio, suave e justa.
As lanternas piscam, lançando luz no ar,
Suas mangas como rios, fluindo livres,
Cada passo uma canção, uma oração, uma alma exposta,
Enquanto o tempo se dobra e os sonhos tomam os céus.
O ar é denso com incenso, quente e profundo,

Um perfume de graça, de verdade, do que buscamos,
Enquanto as sombras se alongam, como sussurros a guardar,
E as estrelas acima se curvam, suas vozes tímidas.
Kyoto, nesta noite, tão suave, tão brilhante,
A beleza de Maiko brilha, um farol, uma luz.

(Kyoto 2013.04.21)

18. Matcha

A sip of matcha, its warmth unfolds
like a hope never asked,
I feel its green pulse rise through my chest,
a quiet rebellion against the cold.
We sit here—two women,
our voices weaving the fabric of time
while Hiei Mountain watches us,
its silence older than our thoughts.
How strange it is, to speak of children
who are not yet born,
of the skin that thins with age,
the body breaking down,
each cell a confession we never planned to make.
The autumn settles around us,
tender, as if it too understands
the weight of what we carry—
this friendship, a delicate thread
between moments that will soon dissolve
like the green of tea into our souls.
There is a truth here,
in the way we talk,
and yet the truth slips away,
leaving only the hum of the mountain,
the fleeting warmth between our hands,

We speak of the future,
and what can we know of it?
It is like this tea—so alive in the moment,
and then, only a memory
we'll never quite taste again.
We hold each other in the quiet
that comes after words,
and the wind moves in,
but we remain.
For now,
we remain.

Matcha

Um gole de matcha, seu calor se desdobra
como uma resposta a uma pergunta nunca feita,
sinto seu pulso verde subir pelo meu peito,
uma rebelião silenciosa contra o frio.
Sentamos aqui—duas mulheres,
nossas vozes tecendo o tecido do tempo
enquanto o Monte Hiei nos observa,
seu silêncio mais antigo que nossos pensamentos.
Que estranho é falar de filhos
que ainda não nasceram,
da pele que enfraquece com a idade,
do corpo que se desfaz,
cada célula uma confissão que nunca planejamos fazer.

O outono se acomoda ao nosso redor,

tênue, como se ele também entendesse

o peso do que carregamos—

essa amizade, um fio delicado

entre momentos que logo se dissolverão

como o verde do chá em nossas almas.

Há uma verdade aqui,

na maneira como falamos,

e ainda assim, a verdade escapa,

deixando apenas o zumbido da montanha,

o calor fugaz entre nossas mãos,

a promessa do agora,

antes que ele se vá.

Falamos sobre o futuro,

e o que podemos saber dele?

É como este chá—tão vivo no momento,

e então, apenas uma memória

que nunca conseguiremos saborear novamente.

Nos mantemos na quietude

que vem depois das palavras,

e o vento entra,

mas permanecemos.

Por agora,

permanecemos.

(Oike - Kyoto 2010.03.23)

19. Thousand gates

In this winter night,
when the world feels heavy and cold,
there is a fire inside us,
a light that will not die.
We are never alone, no.
The spirit walks with us,
guiding our steps through shadows,
through the fear, through the pain.
Faith is not escape—it is strength,
a power that rises when we fall.
Hope opens a thousand gates,
leading us higher,
always higher,
until we reach the light.
We are not lost,
we are becoming—
and in the rising,
we find our way home.

Mil portões

No silêncio da noite,
quando o mundo parece pesado e frio,
há um fogo dentro de nós,

uma luz que não se apaga.
Nunca estamos sozinhos, não.
O espírito caminha conosco,
guiando nossos passos através das sombras,
através do medo, através da dor.
A fé não é fuga—é força,
um poder que se ergue quando caímos.
A esperança abre mil portões,
nos levando mais alto,
sempre mais alto,
até alcançarmos a luz.
Não estamos perdidos,
estamos nos tornando—
e ao nos erguer,
encontramos o nosso caminho de volta para casa.

(Fujiminari - Kyoto 2011.12.22)

20. Gaijin in Kyoto

Where there's light,
There was darkness,
and inside that darkness—
loneliness.
Probably fear too, but who cares?
Because loneliness, even when you're alone,
carries its own damn weight,
like a rock in your chest.
Where there's love,
There was indifference,
silent tears nobody hears,
the numbness that comes with too many drinks,
and a face that's been punched by the years,
marked with the innocence
of someone who never really knew
what it felt like to be loved.
Where there's tomorrow,
There was yesterday,
dust on the picture frames,
mold in the closet.
A burst of joy that's faded,
colors turning to gray.
And now?
Now it's just space—

empty and cold,
with no arms to hold you,
just spores growing in the quiet.
Where there are dreams,
There was night,
and there were nightmares,
a shattered face in the mirror,
too scared to meet its own eyes.
But don't give up,
even if you're lost in the damn loneliness,
and the pain feels like it's eating you alive.
Because deep down,
somewhere in the mess,
you'll find out—
love's the only thing that can patch up all these wounds,
slow and painful,
but it works.

21. Roots and Rhythms

In the colorful days of autumn,
My body tired yet awake,
Despair ripened like fruit on the vine,
While the green fades from the fields,
And the inorganic absence of my father
Lingers like a shadow in the wind.
Rhythmic fractions have taught me to change,
Fixed points where I start to wander,
Seasons of time and place
Questioning why I refuse to leave,
Why I persist in staying.
These are the days of soft breeze and warm sun,
The fragrance of earth kissing my dreams,
When I grow, I want to be strong and bold,
Strong and brave like my Grandma,
Strong and wise like my Mum,
Strong and gentle like my Sis.
I want to cultivate a garden in my city's heart,
And embrace the earth that took me in,
That called me daughter and held me close.

Raizes e Ritmos

Nos dias coloridos do outono

Meu corpo cansado acorda,

Desesperanças que amadureceram,

Enquanto o verde finda nos campos,

A inorgânica ausência de meu pai.

Rítmicas frações me ensinando a mudar,

Pontos fixos onde começo a viajar,

Estações de tempo e de lugar

Interrogam-me por que insisto em ficar.

Estes são dias de brisa e sol brando,

Perfume da terra abraçando meu sonho.

Quando crescer, quero ser forte e não ter medo.

Ser forte e corajosa como minha avó,

Ser forte e sabia como minha mãe,

Ser forte e suave como minha irmã.

Quero fazer um jardim na cidade onde nasci,

E abraçar a terra que me recebeu como filha.

(Yasaka Jinja 2019.11.13)